A DAY in the LIFE OF...

A FIREFIGHTER

Written by Noah Leatherland

Enslow PUBLISHING

Published in 2025 by Enslow Publishing, LLC
2544 Clinton Street
Buffalo, NY 14224

Written by:
Noah Leatherland

Edited by:
Rebecca Phillips-Bartlett

Designed by:
Amelia Harris

Cataloging-in-Publication Data
Names: Leatherland, Noah, 1999-.
Title: A firefighter / Noah Leatherland.
Description: Buffalo, NY : Enslow Publishing, 2025. | Series: A day in the life of... | Includes glossary and index.
Identifiers: ISBN 9781978541832 (pbk.) | ISBN 9781978541849 (library bound) | ISBN 9781978541856 (ebook)
Subjects: LCSH: Fire fighters--Juvenile literature.
Classification: LCC HD8039.F5 L43 2025 | DDC 628.9'2023--dc23

Manufactured in the United States of America

CPSIA compliance information: Batch #CW25ENS: For further information contact Enslow Publishing LLC at 1-800-398-2504.

Image Credits

All images are courtesy of Shutterstock.com, unless otherwise specified. With thanks to Getty Images, Thinkstock Photo and iStockphoto. Recurring – Lee Charlie, TWINS DESIGN STUDIO, RoseRodionova, Drazen Zigic, Dualororua, VAKS-Stock Agency. Cover – HappyPictures. 2–3 – Henrik Dolle. 4–5 – Studio Romantic, PeopleImages.com - Yuri A. 6–7 – Marti Bug Catcher, Sergey Nemirovsky. 8–9 – Tyler Olson. 10–11 – arm315. 12–13 – Henrik Dolle, Gaidamashchuk, Meowu. 14–15 – Matt Gush. 16–17 – Frame Stock Footage. 18–19 – Daniel Avram, SofiaV. 20–21 – LightField Studios, wavebreakmedia, daddy.icon. 22–23 – VAKS-Stock Agency.

CONTENTS

Words that look like this can be found in the glossary on page 24.

A DAY IN THE LIFE

What do you want to do when you grow up? There are so many different jobs that you could do. Some jobs might not quite be how you imagine them.

Nurse

Police officer

A firefighter is someone who puts out fires and helps to keep their community safe. However, there are many other parts of the job you might not think about.

STARTING THE DAY

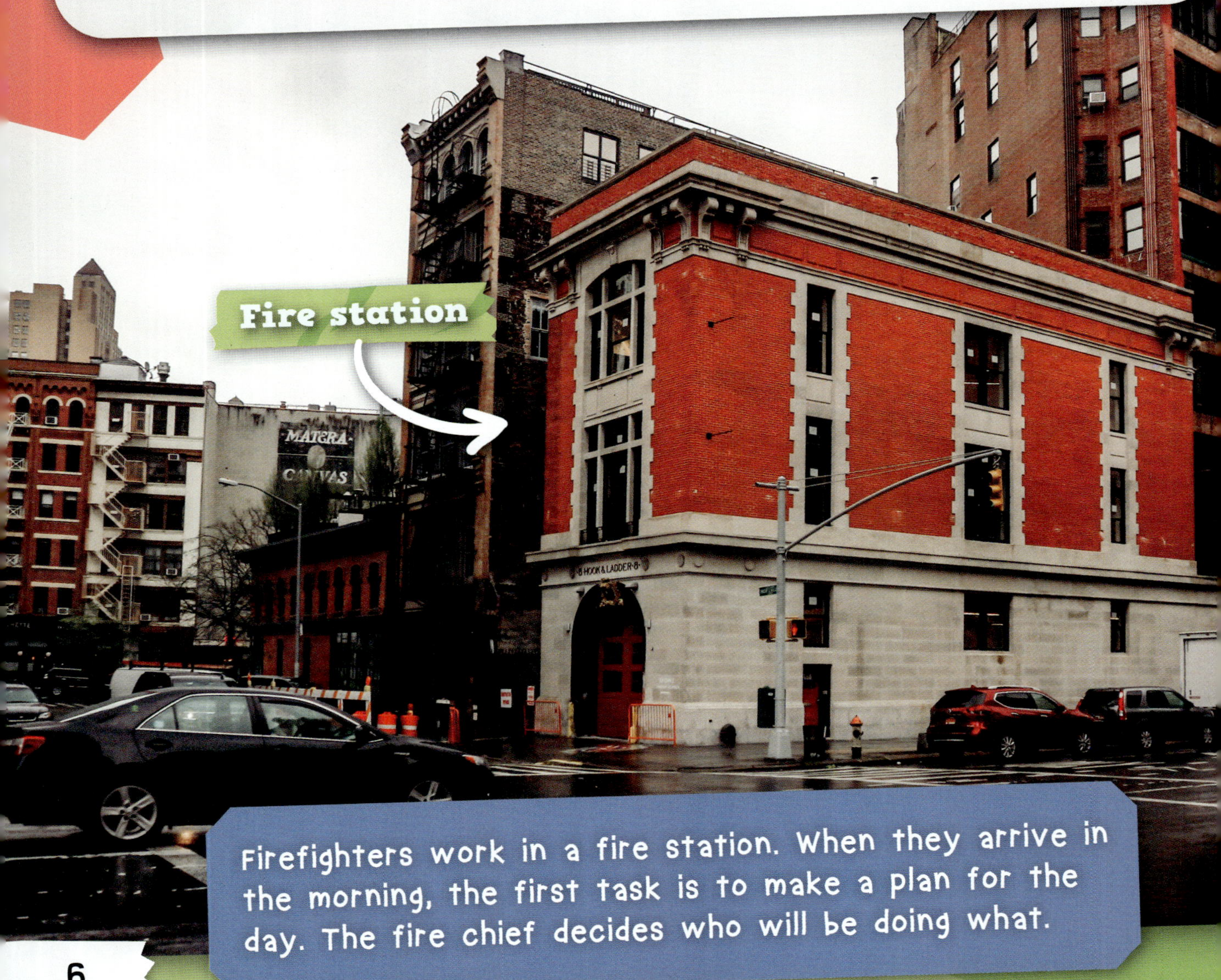

Firefighters work in a fire station. When they arrive in the morning, the first task is to make a plan for the day. The fire chief decides who will be doing what.

Although firefighters make a plan, they know that it could change. They may get called to an emergency at any time. Firefighters are always ready to go if the alarm sounds.

CHECKING EQUIPMENT

Firefighters use a lot of special equipment in their jobs. They need to act quickly whenever they get called to an emergency, so they need to make sure all the equipment is working properly.

Fire engines have a lot of room to store equipment. Some of the equipment is used to put out fires, such as hoses. There is also safety equipment, including masks and other breathing apparatus.

EXERCISING

Firefighters need to keep fit. Their protective gear is heavy, and so is a lot of the equipment. They need to stay strong and healthy so they can move in their gear and carry their equipment.

Firefighters spend some time exercising every day. Many fire stations have gym equipment that the firefighters can use. A good level of fitness keeps firefighters able to do their jobs properly.

TRAINING

Firefighters are always practicing and learning the best ways to put out fires. They might go to training centers where they can practice saving people and putting out fires safely.

Firefighters need to know a lot about the science of fire.

Firefighters go through drills. Drills simulate emergencies that firefighters might get called to. This means they can learn how to deal with different incidents so they are ready when the incidents happen in real life.

EMERGENCY!

When there is an emergency, firefighters need to get there as soon as possible. They put on their gear and jump into the fire engine as quickly as they can.

The firefighters get told about the incident while they are on the way. They decide what tasks everyone will do so they are ready to jump out and help right away.

HERE TO HELP

There are many different incidents that firefighters get called to. However, firefighters have been trained to know how to handle every kind of incident. They know how to keep themselves and others safe.

Firefighters care for people even after they have gotten them to safety. Firefighters are trained to help people who are upset or scared from the incidents. Firefighters need to be kind and friendly.

WHAT STARTED THE FIRE?

Firefighters use their knowledge of fire science to investigate.

A firefighter's job is not over when the incident is cleared up and everyone is safe. They investigate the area to find out what caused the fire.

Firefighters might work with the police to find out what happened. They might help gather evidence. Some things might even need to be tested at a laboratory.

IN THE COMMUNITY

Firefighters do a lot in their community. They go to businesses and help them with fire prevention. Firefighters help businesses make evacuation plans and talk to them about fire safety.

Firefighters also visit schools to teach children and teachers about fire safety. They talk about how to prevent fires and what you should do if you see a fire.

WOULD YOU LIKE TO BE A FIREFIGHTER?

A firefighter's day involves many different tasks. Firefighters spend time training and learning the best ways to fight fires. They need to know how all of their equipment works and how to take care of it.

An emergency can happen at any time of the day. Firefighters need to be ready whenever they get the call for help.

Would you like to be a firefighter?

GLOSSARY

BREATHING APPARATUS	items that help someone breathe in difficult conditions
COMMUNITY	a group of people who live and work in the same place
EQUIPMENT	items that are needed to complete a certain job
EVACUATION	the process of clearing an area or place, getting everybody outside and to safety
EVIDENCE	something that gives proof and can be used to give reason to believe in something
INCIDENTS	events where something has happened
INVESTIGATE	to look into something to find out the truth
LABORATORY	a place where scientists carry out experiments and research
PREVENTION	steps taken to stop something from happening
SIMULATE	to copy the conditions of an event

INDEX